Reading for Comprehension

Level **F**

To the Student

This book contains exciting articles for you to read and enjoy. They tell about real-life adventures, unusual animals, famous people, interesting places, and important events.

There are questions after each article to help you think about and remember what you have read. The last question will give you a chance to write about the topic of the article.

Comprehension means "understanding." Good readers comprehend what they read. You can become a better reader and writer as you go through this book and focus on understanding.

Continental Press

Elizabethtown, PA 17022

Credits

Editorial Development: Matt Baker, Beth Spencer

Editorial Support: Joyce Ober, Anthony Moore

Cover and Interior Design: Joan Herring

Illustrators: Pages 6,7; 36, 37; 42, 43; 48, 49; 52, 53; 56, 57; 92, 93
Margaret Lindmark; Pages 8, 9; 30, 31; 38, 39; 50, 51; 60, 61; 70, 71;
88, 89 Rob Williams

Photo Credits: Front cover: *Bald eagle, saguaro cactus, giraffes:*
www.photos.com; *clownfish:* www.istockphoto.com/redtwiggy; *Mt. Rushmore:*
www.istockphoto.com/megasquib; *open book:* www.istockphoto.com/mstay;
Pages 4, 5: NASA Johnson Space Center – Earth Sciences and Image Analysis;
Pages 10, 11: www.istockphoto.com/TerryHealy; Pages 12, 13:
www.wikipedia.org; Pages 14, 15: www.istockphoto.com/EEI-Tony; Pages 16,
17: www.wikipedia.org; Pages 18, 19: www.photos.com; Pages 20, 21: Library
of Congress Prints and Photographs Division, LC-DIG-matpc-13011; Pages
22, 23: www.wikipedia.org; Pages 26, 27: www.photos.com; Pages 28, 29:
Library of Congress Prints and Photographs Division, LC-USZ62-20901; Pages
32, 33: Library of Congress Prints and Photographs Division, LC-USZ62-
109426; Pages 34, 35: www.photos.com; Pages 44, 45: Library of Congress
Prints and Photographs Division, LC-USZ62-76777; Pages 46, 47:
www.istockphoto.com/atozwebs; Pages 54, 55: www.istockphoto.com/
JordiDelgado; Pages 58, 59: NASA/JPL-Caltech; Pages 62, 63:
www.istockphoto.com/jeridu; Pages 64, 65: www.wikipedia.org; Pages 72, 73:
www.wikipedia.org; Pages 74, 75: www.wikipedia.org; Pages 76, 77: Library
of Congress Prints and Photographs Division, LC-USZ62-105377; Pages 78,
79: www.istockphoto.com/imv; Pages 82, 83: www.istockphoto.com/
davisdezigns; Pages 84, 85: Library of Congress Prints and Photographs
Division, LC-DIG-ppprs-00368; Pages 86, 87: www.photos.com; Pages 90, 91:
www.wikipedia.org; Pages 94, 95: www.istockphoto.com/Caziopeia

ISBN 978-0-8454-1685-3

Circle the correct answer for questions 1–5.
Write your answer to question 6 on a separate piece of paper.

1. The real Dracula _____.
   A was a vampire
   B slept in a coffin
   C could turn into a bat
   D lived near Transylvania

2. Which word in paragraph 2 means "terrible"?
   A Vlad
   B awful
   C feared
   D dragon

3. Which paragraph tells what the name "Dracula" means?
   A 1
   B 2
   C 4
   D 5

4. You can conclude from the article that _____.
   A Prince Vlad was a good ruler
   B horror movies usually tell the truth about history
   C vampires can turn into bats because their parents are dragons
   D Count Dracula is based on a mix of history, myth, and imagination

5. *Inspired* can have the following meanings. Mark the meaning used in paragraph 1.
   A caused
   B artistic
   C very good
   D motivated

6. Write your own Dracula short story. Include details from the article you just read.

Where can you see a coyote?

1   Many people know coyotes as wild dogs that howl and chase road runners in the desert. You can see and hear them in movies and cartoons. The truth, though, is that coyotes do not only live in the desert.

2   Once, coyotes were only found in the northwestern United States. Over the past 200 years, their range has grown. Now they live in every state but Hawaii. Recently one was caught in Central Park in the middle of New York City! Another kind of wild dog, the wolf, has mostly been wiped out, but coyotes are in more and more places all the time.

3   So, since coyotes might be right down the street, why haven't you seen any? And why have they been able to survive when wolves have not? There are a number of things about coyotes that have allowed them to flourish. Coyotes are very adaptable. That is, they learn how to survive in a wide variety of situations. They can eat anything from small animals to fruit to garbage. They do not often eat road runners, but they can.

4   Coyotes are afraid of humans. This is another reason that they have survived in the human world. They can avoid people because they are very smart and have strong senses of sight, smell, and hearing. Though some people do not like coyotes, it is hard to shoot an animal that they cannot find. So, though you can see a coyote anywhere from the deep woods to the middle of a city, you probably will not.

Circle the correct answer for questions 1–5.
Write your answer to question 6 on a separate piece of paper.

1. One reason that coyotes have survived is that _____.
   A they only live in places where there are no people
   B there are lots of road runners for them to eat
   C everyone likes them
   D they are very smart

2. Which word in paragraph 3 means "do well"?
   A adaptable
   B flourish
   C survive
   D learn

3. Which paragraph tells where coyotes live?
   A 1
   B 2
   C 3
   D 4

4. You can infer from the article that _____.
   A coyotes love people
   B coyotes do not live in deserts
   C wolves are not as adaptable as coyotes
   D watching cartoons is a good way to learn about coyotes

5. *Range* can have the following meanings. Mark the meaning used in paragraph 2.
   A cooking stove
   B things in a line
   C place to practice shooting
   D region where animals live

6. Based on what you read about the coyote, write a set of instructions for how you might go about catching one.

What are the Dead Sea Scrolls?

1 The Dead Sea is a saltwater lake located between Israel and Jordan, not far from Jerusalem. In 1947, an Arab shepherd was searching the area for a stray goat. As he looked inside one cave, he discovered some scrolls wrapped in cloth and placed in jars. The scrolls were covered with writing he did not recognize. They meant nothing to the shepherd, so he sold them.

2 Once scholars saw the scrolls, however, they became very excited. The writings were from long ago. Archaeologists, scientists who study ancient people, began exploring all the caves nearby. More scrolls were found, and scholars came from all over the world to study them. These writings are called the Dead Sea Scrolls. Some are quite long. Most, though, are only fragments, often no larger than postage stamps.

3 It is the job of scholars to piece these bits together and make sense of them. The scrolls are mostly religious writings in Hebrew, Greek, and Aramaic, an ancient language that is no longer spoken. It's hard to find the dates and authors of the scrolls. Scientists do know that the scrolls were placed in the caves at different times many hundreds of years ago. Among them are the oldest known copies of the Old Testament.

4 Not all the scrolls are religious. One is a record of treasure deposited throughout the area. Scientists couldn't tell if this record was meant to fool people, or if it was real. Now, however, the scroll itself is a treasure, along with all the other Dead Sea Scrolls.

Circle the correct answer for questions 1–5.
Write your answer to question 6 on a separate piece of paper.

1. The article does *not* tell _____.
   A   how many scrolls were found
   B   where the scrolls were found
   C   when the scrolls were found
   D   what the scrolls contained

2. Which word in paragraph 2 means "parts broken off and incomplete"?
   A   fragments
   B   scholars
   C   stamps
   D   scrolls

3. Which paragraph tells about the languages the scrolls are written in?
   A   1
   B   2
   C   3
   D   4

4. You can conclude from the article that the Dead Sea Scrolls _____.
   A   will never be found again
   B   don't have much historical value
   C   have authors and dates clearly marked
   D   can be used to study the religion of the time

5. *Sense* can have the following meanings. Mark the meaning used in paragraph 3.
   A   one of the ways people learn, like touch and smell
   B   a definite impression or feeling
   C   intelligence
   D   meaning

6. Write a one- or two-paragraph summary of the article you just read.

Why is a moth attracted to light?

1   Have you ever seen a moth bumping against a lighted window? It seems to be knocking itself out trying to get to the light inside. Or have you watched a moth flutter around a lighted candle in dizzy circles? It may fly into the flame and burn. Why?

2   A moth is really an excellent navigator. It doesn't often crash into things. The moth flies in a straight line, using the rays of the sun or moon as guides. These rays are nearly parallel to each other when they reach the earth. The moth positions its body in flight so that the parallel rays always fall on its eyes at a certain angle.

3   The moth has a problem, though, when another light appears nearby. The source of light may be a streetlight, a candle, or a lighted window. When these rays fall on the moth's eyes, the insect changes course automatically. But the artificial light rays are not parallel. They spread out in different directions. To keep them falling on its eyes at the usual angle, the moth must continue changing course. It tilts its body toward the light and goes into a circling flight path. The circles grow smaller and smaller. Finally the confused moth flies into the light or flame. It was never attracted to the light. In fact, the moth was distracted by it.

Circle the correct answer for questions 1–5.
Write your answer to question 6 on a separate piece of paper.

1. A moth positions its body in flight so that _____.
   A it can see the sun
   B it can change course
   C its wings always stay dry
   D light rays hit its eyes at a certain angle

2. Which word in paragraph 3 means "without thinking"?
   A automatically
   B attracted
   C artificial
   D parallel

3. What will *not* happen when a light source appears to a moth?
   A The moth gets scared and flies away.
   B The moth flies into the light.
   C The moth changes course.
   D The moth tilts its body.

4. What is the main idea of the article?
   A A moth is an excellent navigator.
   B A moth positions its body in flight.
   C A moth is distracted by light and changes course to adjust to the rays.
   D A moth becomes confused and gets dizzy flying around a light or flame.

5. You can conclude from the article that moths _____.
   A all die in flames
   B never crash in the daytime
   C try to get away from the light
   D cannot navigate in total darkness

6. How would you "redesign" a moth so it wouldn't be distracted by artificial light? What would the "new and improved" moth do as it flies?

What was the Trojan horse?

1   An ancient poem tells the story of the Trojan War. In it, a Trojan prince fell in love with the wife of a Greek king and fled with her to Troy. To get her back, the Greeks went to war against Troy. But the walled city was strong, and the war went on for ten years. Finally, the Greeks pretended to give up. Leaving a huge wooden horse at Troy's gates, they sailed out of sight. The thankful Trojans brought the gift into their city. At night, men hidden inside the horse crept out. They opened the gates and let in the Greek soldiers. Because of this trick, Troy was finally conquered.

2   Is this old tale true? No Trojan horse has ever been found anywhere. But in the 1870s, the remains of Troy were discovered in Turkey. As archaeologists dug through the ruins, they found many layers. They concluded that Troy had risen and fallen many times over thousands of years. What had made it such an important place?

3   The answer is Troy's location. It was near the Dardanelles, a strait between the Mediterranean and Black seas. The current there is very strong. To sail against it, ships had to wait until the wind was behind them. Sometimes the sailors waited for weeks. Meanwhile, Troy demanded heavy tolls from them. Whenever the Greeks got tired of making the payments, they would fight instead. So the Trojan War was probably fought many times. And it was because of money—not a woman.

24   **Reading for Comprehension**

Circle the correct answer for questions 1–5.
Write your answer to question 6 on a separate piece of paper.

1. Troy was located _____.
   A in Greece
   B in Turkey
   C on an island
   D in the mountains

2. Which word in paragraph 3 means "a narrow body of water"?
   A location
   B current
   C strait
   D tolls

3. The Trojan War was most likely caused by _____.
   A a huge wooden horse
   B the wife of a Greek king
   C heavy tolls on the Greeks
   D a strong current near Troy

4. According to an ancient poem, what happened first in the Trojan War?
   A The Greeks declared war against Troy.
   B The Greeks left a wooden horse at Troy's gates.
   C Men opened the gates and let in Greek soldiers.
   D A Trojan prince fled to Troy with the wife of a Greek king.

5. You can conclude from the article that the Trojan War _____.
   A did not last long
   B did not really happen
   C pitted brother against brother
   D happened thousands of years ago

6. Imagine you are a Greek soldier. Write your own tale describing what it was like to hide in the wooden horse. What happened when you were released?

Why do animals play?

1   You probably laugh at kittens playing. They pounce on leaves or chase after one another. They knock one another over and nip at necks and tails. And you think to yourself, "Aren't they cute?" But these young animals are really going to "school" while they play. At a time when their brains are growing, play helps the brain send messages to the muscles. It strengthens balance and muscle control. In play, baby animals practice behaviors they'll need as adults.

2   These behaviors are not as important in animals kept as pets. But in the wild, behaviors learned in play can mean the difference between life and death. For instance, lambs or baby deer may suddenly bolt and run off across a meadow or through a forest for no clear reason. They are actually practicing a behavior that might save them from a wolf or mountain lion later on.

3   Wolf and lion cubs, too, need to practice. They pretend to hunt. They carefully stalk their "prey." Then they pounce, nipping and pawing at something until they've "captured" it. If these baby animals don't learn how to hunt when they're young, they may not be able to feed themselves as adults.

4   Play is especially important for animals that live in groups. Some baby monkeys spend as much as half their waking hours in play. They are learning how to "win" and "lose" games and make-believe fights. But they are also learning how to get along with other members of their group. So the next time you see young animals playing, remember, it's not all play.

Circle the correct answer for questions 1–5.
Write your answer to question 6 on a separate piece of paper.

1. Baby animals that eat meat _____.
   A live a long time
   B learn how to swim
   C practice hunting skills
   D run away in fright from other animals

2. Which word in paragraph 1 means "actions that living things do at certain times"?
   A brains
   B leaves
   C messages
   D behaviors

3. Which paragraph tells about the play of monkeys?
   A 1
   B 2
   C 3
   D 4

4. What is the main idea of the article?
   A Play is not important to animals kept as pets.
   B Play is important to animals that live in groups.
   C Baby animals play to strengthen balance and muscle control.
   D Baby animals play to practice behaviors they'll need as adults.

5. *Bolt* can have the following meanings. Mark the meaning used in paragraph 2.
   A to dart off
   B a metal pin
   C a lightning stroke
   D to swallow without chewing

6. Write a letter to the staff at a local zoo to explain the importance of animal play. Suggest ways they might set up the living area of baby animals.

Who was Amelia Earhart?

1   Amelia Earhart became interested in flying when the airplane was still a fairly new invention. She worked hard to earn money for flying lessons. And soon her knowledge and handling of planes earned her the respect of other aviators.

2   In 1932, Amelia became the first woman to fly across the Atlantic Ocean alone. Her solo flight took a great deal of courage. In the middle of the ocean, she ran into a terrible storm. The plane began shaking violently. Because the instrument that measured altitude was broken, Amelia had no way of knowing how high she was flying. If she tried to fly below the storm, she might plunge into the ocean. So she decided to fly above it. The higher the plane climbed, the colder the air became. Ice formed on the wings. The plane went into a spin. It spun downward for thousands of feet. Luckily, warmer air on the way down melted the ice. Amelia was able to level the plane just above the waves. With her engine in flames, Amelia pressed on, finally landing safely in Ireland.

3   This nearly tragic experience did not keep Amelia from flying. The daring pilot went on to set other records. Then in 1937 she began an exciting trip around the world. This flight, however, did not end well. All contact with the plane was lost as it headed for home. Though searchers have investigated some promising leads, Amelia, her navigator, and the plane have not yet been found.

Circle the correct answer for questions 1–5.
Write your answer to question 6 on a separate piece of paper.

1. Amelia Earhart is famous for being the first woman to _____.
   A have courage
   B ride in an airplane
   C wear aviator sunglasses
   D fly across the Atlantic alone

2. Which word in paragraph 3 means "sad and terrible"?
   A tragic
   B daring
   C exciting
   D promising

3. What happened first in the life of Amelia Earhart?
   A She set flying records.
   B She earned money for flying lessons.
   C She left for a flight around the world.
   D She flew across the Atlantic Ocean alone.

4. You can infer from the article that Amelia Earhart _____.
   A was overly cautious when flying a plane
   B used effective navigation equipment
   C couldn't fly as well as a male pilot
   D is a hero to female pilots

5. *Spin* can have the following meanings. Mark the meaning used in paragraph 2.
   A to turn in circles
   B a fast downward spiral
   C to make thread or yarn
   D a state of mental confusion

6. Little is known about what happened on Amelia Earhart's final flight. Write your own story, written from Amelia's perspective, about what happened the day her plane disappeared.

How can water flow up a tree?

1   According to one law of nature, water flows downhill. Yet water will flow to the top of even the tallest tree. How does this happen?

2   Every day, an enormous amount of water evaporates from the leaves of a tree. This process is called *transpiration.* From there, another law of nature takes over. This law states that water molecules cling together. If one drop finds its way through an opening, others follow. So, as the water evaporates from a tree's leaves, more water moves in to fill the space. Bit by bit, water is pulled upward through the tree.

3   Yet another law of nature is also at work here. On the tree roots, there are thousands of little hairs with tiny cells that hold water. The earth around the roots, though, usually holds more water. This gives the soil a higher pressure. And it is nature's law that water moves from higher pressure areas to lower pressure areas. Water in the soil is forced through the cell walls into the root hair cells. By this process, called *osmosis,* the tree always has a supply of water.

4   Sun, wind, rain, and heat all affect the amount of water in a tree. On a sunny day, a middle-sized oak tree can pull 150 gallons through its trunk. About 95% of this water evaporates. The rest feeds the tree. Between the pull of transpiration and the push of osmosis, the tree gets the water it needs.

Circle the correct answer for questions 1–5.
Write your answer to question 6 on a separate piece of paper.

1. The article does *not* tell about the _____ of a tree.
   A root cells
   B leaves
   C roots
   D bark

2. Which word in paragraph 2 means "quantity"?
   A amount
   B process
   C space
   D law

3. Which paragraph tells what transpiration is?
   A 1
   B 2
   C 3
   D 4

4. What does *not* happen after water evaporates from the leaves of a tree?
   A Water molecules cling together.
   B Water moves in to fill the space.
   C Water moves to a high pressure area.
   D Water in the soil is forced through cell walls.

5. You can conclude from the article that laws of nature can _____.
   A explain human behavior
   B work together
   C save water
   D be useless

6. Write a one- or two-paragraph summary of the article you just read.

Who was Rosa Parks?

1   Rosa Parks became famous for sitting down on a bus. After her death in 2005, she became the first woman to lie in state in the U.S. Capitol. This is a great honor that is usually given to presidents and other important people in government. How did such a simple act make her so important?

2   Rosa Parks grew up in the South at a time when African Americans were treated as second-class citizens. In many states, they were not allowed to vote or even use the same public restrooms as white people. They were forced to sit in the back of buses and give up their seats to white people.

3   One day in 1955, Rosa was riding the bus home from work. A white man told her to get up so that he could have her seat. Instead of doing as he said, though, she stayed where she was. She was arrested and fined for demanding her rights as a person.

4   This was not the end of the story, though. Rosa knew a young preacher named Martin Luther King Jr. In response to Rosa's arrest, he called for a boycott of city buses. African Americans would stop riding the buses until they were allowed to sit wherever they pleased.

5   The boycott lasted for more than a year. In the end, it was a success. It is now considered the start of the Civil Rights movement. Thanks to the actions of Rosa Parks and others like her, the United States has come much closer to being a place where no one is denied equal rights.

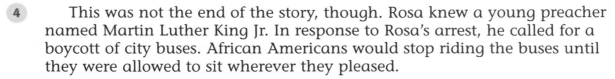

Circle the correct answer for questions 1–5.
Write your answer to question 6 on a separate piece of paper.

1. Rosa Parks was told to give up her seat because _____.

   A she was a woman

   B she had been arrested

   C she was African American

   D she knew Martin Luther King Jr.

2. Which word in paragraph 4 means "refusal to use"?

   A end

   B arrest

   C boycott

   D allowed

3. Which paragraph tells what the South was like when Rosa Parks was growing up?

   A 1

   B 2

   C 3

   D 4

4. Which of these might be another example of being treated like a "second-class citizen"?

   A leading a boycott

   B being convicted of a crime

   C lying in state in the U.S. Capitol

   D being paid less because of nationality

5. *Called* can have the following meanings. Mark the meaning used in paragraph 4.

   A invited to meet

   B gave the order for

   C uttered in a loud voice

   D summoned to employment

6. Choose something that you would like to change in the world and write a letter to the editor of your local newspaper to support your position.

What are the facts about mushrooms?

1. Mushrooms belong to a group of living things called fungi (FUN•jy). There are more than 75,000 types of fungi. Molds and yeasts are two kinds. Mushrooms are fungi with an umbrella shape.

2. Like all fungi, mushrooms have no real roots, leaves, or flowers. They grow from spores instead of seeds. For most mushrooms, the spores are made in thin slits under the mushroom cap and then sent floating through the air like dust. If a spore lands on a good growing spot, it soaks up moisture there. Soon it becomes a mass of white threads that look like roots. This mass feeds on rotting wood, dead leaves, or parts of living trees. It can live hidden under tree bark or under the ground for months or years. When moisture and temperature are just right, mushroom lumps begin to swell on the mass of threads. Finally, they push up through the ground.

3. Mushrooms may be as small as buttons or as big as footballs. They come in all colors, from white and orange to red and black. There are even mushrooms that glow at night. The strange names of different mushrooms give you an idea of their various shapes and effects. There are mushrooms called earth stars, jack o'lanterns, death caps, and destroying angels.

4. Some mushrooms may be eaten safely. Others are poisonous. Yet there is no easy way to tell them apart. In fact, deadly mushrooms often taste delicious. You must learn from books or people exactly which mushrooms are safe and which are not. Never eat a wild mushroom unless you are sure it is harmless. A mistake could be fatal.

Circle the correct answer for questions 1–5.
Write your answer to question 6 on a separate piece of paper.

1. The article does *not* tell about the _____ of mushrooms.
   A sizes
   B stems
   C colors
   D names

2. Which word in paragraph 2 means "a large group of things in a small, tight space"?
   A cap
   B slits
   C mass
   D spore

3. Which paragraph tells how many kinds of fungi there are?
   A 1
   B 2
   C 3
   D 4

4. What happens last in the life cycle of a mushroom?
   A A spore becomes a mass of white threads that look like roots.
   B White threads live hidden under tree bark or underground.
   C A spore lands on a growing spot and soaks up moisture.
   D Lumps begin to swell on a mass of white threads.

5. You can infer from the article that mushrooms _____.
   A are never safe
   B have a sour taste
   C can't grow in deserts
   D have not been studied much

6. How are mushrooms like plants? How are they different?

What language do deaf people use?

1   Deaf people around the world communicate in sign language. But that doesn't mean that a deaf German and a deaf American could understand each other. They would probably sign in different languages. About 50 sign languages have developed naturally in countries around the world.

2   In the United States, deaf people use American Sign Language. ASL is not signed English. In that system, gestures stand for whole words. But deaf people often don't use signed English because they think it is clumsy and artificial. In contrast, ASL is a true language.

3   What are the characteristics of a true language? First of all, it is made up of small symbols or sounds. These have no meaning by themselves, but they can be combined into meaningful units. Think of the sounds and letters of the alphabet and how they are connected to make spoken or written words. Second, a real language has grammar, rules for putting words together. Finally, a natural language changes over time.

4   ASL has all these characteristics. It uses the hands, face, and body together in motion to create meaning. The shapes of the hands are just one element of a sign. Where and how the hands move in relation to the body or face is another. The expression on the face is also important. For example, tilting the head forward and raising the eyebrows while signing turns a statement into a question. And like English, ASL is always changing. In particular, ASL constantly adds new signs in an attempt to keep up with constantly changing technology.

Circle the correct answer for questions 1–5.
Write your answer to question 6 on a separate piece of paper.

1. Deaf people in America do *not* often use _____.
    A   American Sign Language
    B   good grammar
    C   signed English
    D   their hands

2. Which word in paragraph 3 means "special features"?
    A   characteristics
    B   symbols
    C   sounds
    D   units

3. Which paragraph tells about true languages?
    A   1
    B   2
    C   3
    D   4

4. You can conclude from the article that American Sign Language _____.
    A   is used throughout the world
    B   is very similar to signed English
    C   is comfortable for deaf people to use
    D   is impossible for hearing people to learn

5. *Stand* can have the following meanings. Mark the meaning used in paragraph 2.
    A   to be upright on one's feet
    B   a table to sell things
    C   to put up with
    D   to represent

6. How is the language you speak with friends different from the language you use with adults? Compare the two kinds of language and give examples of each.

How does an IMAX movie work?

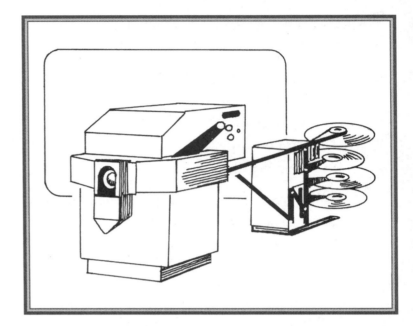

1. You are making your way up Mount Everest. It's been a hard and dangerous climb. The peak looms above you. You pause to put on your oxygen mask. All you can see are snow and ice and sky. Of course, you're not really on Mount Everest. You're only watching a movie. But what a movie it is! The screen is eight stories high. The picture is unbelievably clear. The sound is so realistic you can almost feel the wind. That's the way it is in an IMAX theater.

2. Many kinds of technology help make the IMAX experience so powerful. Let's start with the film. Each frame, or picture, is about ten times larger than regular movie film. So, it can hold that much more detail, color, and depth. It moves through the projector twice as fast as ordinary film. This speed makes the movie seem even more lifelike.

3. In ordinary projectors, film is held against the lens by friction. In an IMAX projector, it is held by a vacuum. Film moves horizontally through the projector in a smooth wavelike motion. The result is a steady picture that is always sharp and clear.

4. The IMAX screen may be up to 80 feet high. It is set at a special angle and painted to give the most reflection. There are six channels of sound. They are balanced so that the sound is the same everywhere in the theater. The screen and seats are designed to prevent echoing.

5. The first permanent IMAX theater opened in Toronto, Canada, in 1971. Today there are IMAX theaters across the United States and in many other countries.

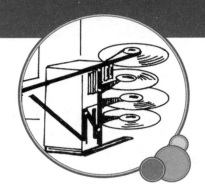

Circle the correct answer for questions 1–5.
Write your answer to question 6 on a separate piece of paper.

1. IMAX film has a picture area about _____ times bigger than ordinary movie film.

   A 2

   B 6

   C 8

   D 10

2. Which word in paragraph 2 means "a system using special tools and methods"?

   A technology

   B projector

   C detail

   D frame

3. Which paragraph tells how IMAX projectors are different from other movie projectors?

   A 1

   B 2

   C 3

   D 4

4. The steady, sharp picture in an IMAX movie is caused by _____.

   A the size of the film

   B the angle and color of the screen

   C film moving fast through the projector

   D film moving smoothly through the projector

5. *Sharp* can have the following meanings. Mark the meaning used in paragraph 3.

   A clear in detail

   B keen in intellect

   C marked by anger

   D having a thin edge

6. Think of a movie that you would like to see in an IMAX theater. Explain why the movie would be good in this format.

Is the Atlantic Ocean getting smaller?

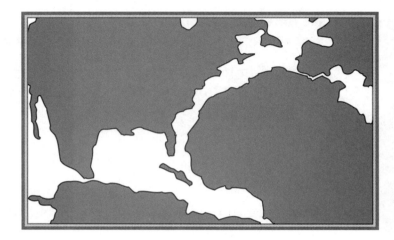

1   Many scientists believe that all the land on Earth was part of one big landmass 300 million years ago. Then about 200 million years ago, the landmass started to break up into five continents. The continents began drifting apart very slowly until they ended up where they are today. The huge ditch that was formed between some of the continents slowly filled with water and became the Atlantic Ocean. Scientists call this theory continental drift.

2   Continents move because the center of the Earth is very hot. The Earth's core is made up of liquid rock that the continents float on. From time to time, this hot, molten material breaks through the rock above it. A volcano is the result. When the volcano is on the ocean floor, the water cools the molten lava into rock again. As the lava cools and becomes part of the Earth's crust, it pushes the rock around it farther and farther apart.

3   Today, there are many active volcanoes in the deepest parts of the Pacific Ocean. Every year, more and more new crust forms. This is slowly making the Pacific Ocean bigger. At the same time, the Atlantic Ocean is slowly getting smaller because the continents are being pushed toward each other on that side of the world.

4   This drift is exactly the opposite of what happened 200 million years ago. The process is so slow that people don't notice it. But if people are still living in New York City in another 200 million years, they might be able to drive to Africa by car.

Circle the correct answer for questions 1–5.
Write your answer to question 6 on a separate piece of paper.

1. If scientists are right, New York will be connected to _____ in 200 million years.

    A   Africa

    B   China

    C   Europe

    D   Canada

2. Which word in paragraph 2 means "the center"?

    A   material

    B   volcano

    C   lava

    D   core

3. Which paragraph tells why the Pacific Ocean is getting bigger?

    A   1

    B   2

    C   3

    D   4

4. What does *not* happen to make a continent move?

    A   Water cools molten lava into rock.

    B   Lava becomes part of the Earth's crust.

    C   Earth's core cools and remains dormant.

    D   Molten material breaks through the rock above it.

5. *Crust* can have the following meanings. Mark the meaning used in paragraph 2.

    A   the outside part of bread

    B   a hard, outer layer

    C   the shell of a pie

    D   a scab

6. The Hawaiian Islands were formed from volcanoes in the Pacific Ocean. What do you think will happen to them in the next 200 million years? Why do you think that?

What is alchemy?

1   For over a thousand years, people tried to change lead and other common metals into gold and silver. They were practicing a mix of magic, science, and religion called alchemy (AL•kuh•mee). Alchemists believed everything in the world was made up of one basic substance. When this substance was heated, cooled, or dried, it became the four elements of earth, air, fire, and water. Because everything came from one substance, alchemists thought they could change one thing into another by changing the balance of the four elements. Alchemists also thought that the color, shine, and texture of gold were things that could be transferred to other metals.

2   Gold lasts a long time. So many people believed that anyone who could make gold would also learn the secret of living forever. Stories were told about the magic powers of alchemists. To protect their secrets, alchemists wrote in code so no one else could read their writings.

3   Of course, no one ever changed lead into gold. But some dishonest alchemists fooled people. The alchemists used containers with wax bottoms. In them, they hid small pieces of gold. When the container was heated, the wax melted and the gold mixed in with the lead. People watching would think some of the lead had turned to gold. Then they would pay the alchemists money to "make" more gold.

4   Alchemists failed to change metals into gold. But they did add to our knowledge in another way. Their work led to today's science of chemistry.

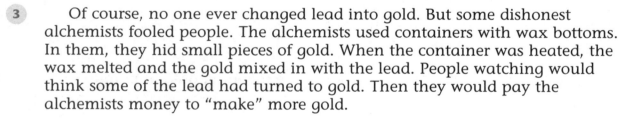

Circle the correct answer for questions 1–5.
Write your answer to question 6 on a separate piece of paper.

1. _____ is *not* one of the four elements.

    A Air

    B Fire

    C Water

    D Electricity

2. Which word in paragraph 1 means "the way something feels"?

    A substance

    B balance

    C texture

    D color

3. Which paragraph tells about the four elements?

    A 1

    B 2

    C 3

    D 4

4. You can conclude from the article that alchemists _____.

    A placed a lot of importance on gold

    B shared their techniques with the public

    C were all honest men with religious beliefs

    D found great wealth because of their practices

5. *Code* can have the following meanings. Mark the meaning used in paragraph 2.

    A statement of law

    B imposed standard

    C system for communication

    D instructions for a computer

6. Imagine you are an alchemist. Write an advertisement to convince people to pay you to change their regular metals to gold.

Reading for Comprehension   43

Who was Alexander Graham Bell?

1　　Alexander Graham Bell is famous for inventing the telephone. But most people don't know that he also invented many other things. Because his mother was deaf, Alexander grew up wanting to help people who couldn't hear. He was also very interested in science. During the day, Bell taught deaf children. At night, he often did experiments with electricity until 4 A.M.

2　　The telegraph had been used for a long time to send messages through a wire. Alexander Graham Bell was the first person to discover that the human voice could also be carried over wire. In 1877 at Salem, Massachusetts, Bell tried his telephone in a room full of people. His assistant, Thomas Watson, read a news story and sang a song over the telephone from Boston, 16 miles away.

3　　Using the same idea as the telephone, Bell invented a machine that could tell if someone had trouble hearing. Wearing earphones, people listened for high and low sounds. Bell also invented a metal detector. At that time, people often died from bullet wounds because doctors couldn't find the bullets. Bell's machine beeped loudly when it got near one.

4　　Alexander Graham Bell continued to work on new ideas until he died. He developed a new kind of boat motor and a way to build stronger houses. He also invented a machine to help people breathe. When someone asked him where he found the time to invent things, Bell said, "A true inventor can't help inventing any more than he can help thinking."

Reading for Comprehension

Circle the correct answer for questions 1–5.
Write your answer to question 6 on a separate piece of paper.

1. The first telephone message came from _____.
   A Salem
   B Boston
   C Vermont
   D New York

2. Which word in paragraph 1 means "operations carried out under controlled conditions"?
   A science
   B invented
   C electricity
   D experiments

3. Which paragraph tells about the first use of the telephone?
   A 1
   B 2
   C 3
   D 4

4. Alexander Graham Bell's desire to invent things began mostly because of _____.
   A deaf children
   B his deaf mother
   C the invention of the telegraph
   D people dying from bullet wounds

5. You can conclude from the article that the telephone _____.
   A was originally invented for deaf people
   B was really invented by Alexander Graham Bell's assistant
   C was just one of Alexander Graham Bell's important inventions
   D was the only invention for which Alexander Graham Bell received recognition

6. Compare Alexander Graham Bell to another inventor in U.S. history. You might compare him to Thomas Edison, who invented the electric light, or to Elias Howe, who invented the sewing machine. Which inventor's work is most important? Why?

Why aren't animals on electric power lines electrocuted?

1.   Twisted metal wires inside power lines carry strong currents of electricity. These deadly currents can electrocute an animal or a person instantly. Yet birds and squirrels can be seen on high wires all the time. Why aren't they killed?

2.   To be electrocuted, an animal has to complete an electrical circuit. It has to act as a link between the electricity and another object. If it is not touching anything except the wire it is on, it is safe.

3.   Birds are seldom electrocuted. They are so small that they hardly ever touch anything besides the wire. But if a bird's tail or wing brushes against something while the bird is perched on a power line, the circuit is completed. The bird gets electrocuted. A squirrel is in even more danger. It is bigger than a bird and has the ability to leap from one wire to another. If its tail touches one line as its feet reach another, the squirrel is killed.

4.   Power lines are usually above the reach of people, but accidents can happen. Sometimes storms knock down lines, or people try to use a pole to get a kite or model airplane caught in a power line. When the circuit is completed, the person is electrocuted.

5.   Electricity is useful, but it must be respected. Birds and squirrels need luck to protect them from it. People can use their heads.

Circle the correct answer for questions 1–5.
Write your answer to question 6 on a separate piece of paper.

1. Animals on power lines are not electrocuted because they _____.
   A are careful
   B don't complete a circuit
   C aren't hurt by electricity
   D know which wire to sit on

2. Which word in paragraph 2 means "complete path of an electric current"?
   A link
   B circuit
   C object
   D electricity

3. Which paragraph tells how people can be accidentally electrocuted?
   A 1
   B 2
   C 3
   D 4

4. If a bird is electrocuted while on a power line, it most likely _____.
   A was chased by a squirrel
   B grasped the wire too tightly
   C touched the wire with its beak
   D brushed against something else

5. *Brushes* can have the following meanings. Mark the meaning used in paragraph 3.
   A things to paint with
   B touches lightly
   C bushy tails
   D shrubs

6. Write a one- or two-paragraph summary of the article you just read.

Who is Spike Lee?

1   Jacqueline Lee could see that her son, Shelton, was tough. That was why she nicknamed him "Spike." Being tough turned out to be a good thing for Spike Lee. He grew up to be one of the most controversial filmmakers of his time.

2   From the start, Spike Lee's movies made some people angry. In 1979, he was one of the few African Americans in film school at New York University. His first-year project was a film called *The Answer.* In it, he attacked a classic film called *Birth of a Nation,* calling it racist. This did not please some of Lee's teachers, but that did not keep him from speaking his mind.

3   In 1989, Lee made *Do the Right Thing.* The movie made him famous but also gained negative attention because of the way it looked at racial issues in New York City. Then in 1992 he made a movie about the civil rights leader Malcolm X. It was a big hit. Its star, Denzel Washington, was nominated for an Academy Award for Best Actor. A movie about a controversial figure such as Malcolm X was bound to get Lee even more attention from the press, and it did.

4   Spike Lee has stayed true to his beliefs and kept on making movies his own way. No matter what anyone says about them or about him, he continues to express the way he sees the world. His 2006 movie *Inside Man* was his biggest hit since *Malcolm X.* Clearly, moviegoers have not seen the last of Spike Lee.

Circle the correct answer for questions 1–5.
Write your answer to question 6 on a separate piece of paper.

1. Spike Lee made all of the following movies *except* _____.
   A *Do the Right Thing*
   B *Birth of a Nation*
   C *Inside Man*
   D *Malcolm X*

2. Which word in paragraph 3 means "causing strong disagreement"?
   A issues
   B bound
   C attention
   D controversial

3. Which paragraph tells how Shelton became known as Spike?
   A 1
   B 2
   C 3
   D 4

4. You can infer from the article that _____.
   A causing trouble is always a good thing
   B Spike Lee has learned not to be controversial
   C Malcolm X did not like the film Spike Lee made about him
   D Spike Lee does not think that being controversial is a bad thing

5. *Press* can have the following meanings. Mark the meaning used in paragraph 3.
   A push
   B squeeze
   C news media
   D printing machine

6. Think of another person who went against what other people thought and had a positive influence on society. What did this person do that is so noteworthy?

How did teddy bears get their name?

1   For more than 100 years teddy bears have been loved by children all over the world. The bears come in many shapes and sizes. Some teddy bears, such as Winnie the Pooh, have even become famous. As it turns out, three different countries—the United States, England, and Germany—claim to have given the teddy bear its name.

2   The best known story comes from the United States. In 1902, President Theodore Roosevelt, whose nickname was "Teddy," went hunting with his friends. They found a bear cub, but because the cub was small and helpless, Teddy refused to shoot it. He would not let anyone else shoot it, either.

3   Soon after this, someone drew a cartoon showing Teddy saving the bear. A husband and wife who owned a store in New York saw it and started to make stuffed bears to sell. They called them "Teddy's Bears." The Germans have a similar story. They say that it was a German company named Steiff that started making and selling the bears in 1903. In England, on the other hand, people say that the bear was named after King Edward VII, whose nickname was also "Teddy."

4   People may never know for sure who gave the teddy bear its name. Wherever the name came from, this furry friend will still be welcome all over the world.

Circle the correct answer for questions 1–5.
Write your answer to question 6 on a separate piece of paper.

1. President Roosevelt and King Edward VII both _____.

   A loved bears

   B started toy companies

   C were nicknamed "Teddy"

   D collected stuffed animals

2. Which word in paragraph 1 means "known far and wide"?

   A claim

   B loved

   C given

   D famous

3. Which paragraph tells about Teddy Roosevelt?

   A 1

   B 2

   C 3

   D 4

4. You can infer from the article that _____.

   A King Edward loved bears

   B Teddy Roosevelt did not like to hunt

   C people in England did not like Teddy Roosevelt

   D teddy bears are popular in the United States, Germany, and England

5. *Saving* can have the following meanings. Mark the meaning used in paragraph 3.

   A protecting

   B keeping

   C hoarding

   D collecting

6. Write your own story to explain how the teddy bear got its name.

Who first learned how to make glass?

1.   In ancient times, people used glass charms to keep away evil spirits. Beads, drinking cups, and other things made of glass have been found in the ruins of past civilizations. How did these people learn to make glass?

2.   Silica sand is a basic ingredient of glass. If it is heated to a high temperature, it melts to form glass. Lightning and volcanoes are hot enough to melt the sand naturally. This is how the first glass was formed. But there is an easier way. Silica sand will melt at a lower temperature if soda is added.

3.   No one knows exactly how people first learned to make glass. It could have happened when someone built a fire on a beach full of silica sand. The fire wouldn't have been hot enough to melt the sand. But suppose the people had used rocks with soda in them to circle their fire. As the fire cooled, the people would have found hard pieces of crude glass.

4.   Glass made from just silica sand and soda will dissolve in water. Luckily, someone found that adding lime keeps glass hard forever. Today people add other things to glass. Some give it color. Others make it bright or strong. There are thousands of formulas for making different kinds of glass. It can be as fragile as crystal or as strong as a car window. Some can even withstand bullets. But all glass must have the three basic ingredients that were put together accidentally thousands of years ago—sand, soda, and lime.

Circle the correct answer for questions 1–5.
Write your answer to question 6 on a separate piece of paper.

1. Sand and soda become hard glass when _____ is added.
    A water
    B silica
    C heat
    D lime

2. Which word in paragraph 4 means "easily broken"?
    A basic
    B hard
    C strong
    D fragile

3. Which paragraph tells what makes glass stay hard forever?
    A 1
    B 2
    C 3
    D 4

4. You can infer from the article that the less lime that is added to glass, the _____.
    A more sturdy the glass is
    B more fragile the glass is
    C more sand the glass needs
    D more soda the glass needs

5. *Charms* can have the following meanings. Mark the meaning used in paragraph 1.
    A pleases
    B traits that delight
    C controls, as a snake
    D things thought to have magic powers

6. The article gives instructions on how to make glass. Think of something you know how to make and write a set of instructions.

How do you grade a stone?

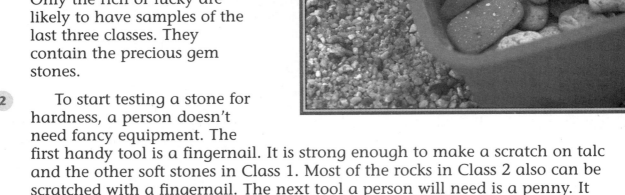

1   If a person finds a stone on the ground, it's not likely that he or she knows how to grade it the way the experts do. They place stones into 10 classes, depending on how hard the stone is. Most stones fit into the first seven classes. Only the rich or lucky are likely to have samples of the last three classes. They contain the precious gem stones.

2   To start testing a stone for hardness, a person doesn't need fancy equipment. The first handy tool is a fingernail. It is strong enough to make a scratch on talc and the other soft stones in Class 1. Most of the rocks in Class 2 also can be scratched with a fingernail. The next tool a person will need is a penny. It will scratch minerals like calcite in Class 3. For Classes 4 and 5, the tool is a pocketknife. For Class 6 rocks, a steel file is needed.

3   Class 7 contains quartz. Quartz is one of the hardest and most common minerals found on Earth. It will scratch all the minerals in the first six classes. It cannot, however, scratch the topaz and other gem stones of Class 8. These can be scratched by the precious sapphire in Class 9.

4   The only mineral that can scratch Class 9 stones is the rare and beautiful diamond. It stands alone in Class 10. Diamonds are so hard that they can cut almost anything. They are even used to drill oil wells. The only natural thing that can scratch a diamond is another diamond.

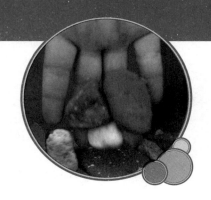

Circle the correct answer for questions 1–5.
Write your answer to question 6 on a separate piece of paper.

1. The hardness of a rock is decided by _____.
   A grinding
   B touching
   C weighing
   D scratching

2. Which word in paragraph 2 means "easy to use"?
   A soft
   B fancy
   C handy
   D strong

3. Which paragraph tells about the hardness of the diamond?
   A 1
   B 2
   C 3
   D 4

4. What is the main idea of the article?
   A Diamonds can cut almost anything.
   B Quartz is one of the most common minerals found on Earth.
   C Stones are graded in ten classes depending on how hard they are.
   D A person doesn't need fancy equipment to test a stone's hardness.

5. You can conclude from the article that a pocketknife will scratch _____.
   A talc
   B topaz
   C quartz
   D sapphire

6. Why would diamonds be used to drill oil wells? Explain why diamonds are used for this and other purposes rather than other rocks or minerals.

Who were the Neanderthals?

1   The bones of Stone Age people are often found in Europe and western Asia. Some skeletons resemble those of modern humans. But the bones of Neanderthals are quite different. A Neanderthal skull has a bulging ridge of bone above the eyes. The chin is very small. The arm and leg bones are very large and heavy. They supported huge muscles. These people were much stronger than the average human is today. A Neanderthal man could have easily lifted hundreds of pounds.

2   Neanderthals were intelligent, too. They had to be to survive in their harsh environment. Neanderthals knew how to make fine stone tools. They were good hunters. With their great strength, they could kill large animals. These early humans lived in small groups and may have had a spoken language. They also buried their dead, something animals don't do.

3   Neanderthals completely vanished about 35,000 years ago. But their disappearance remains a mystery. Did they die out? Were they killed? Did they change into modern humans?

4   Scientists once thought that Neanderthals might be our ancestors. Now they believe these powerful humans were more like cousins than grandparents. The ancestors of modern humans were the Cro-Magnon people, who lived at the same time as the Neanderthals. Did they compete with the Neanderthals? No one is certain. The Cro-Magnons were physically weaker, but they were also very clever and inventive.

Circle the correct answer for questions 1–5.
Write your answer to question 6 on a separate piece of paper.

1. Compared to humans today, Neanderthals were much _____.
   A stronger
   B weaker
   C smarter
   D faster

2. Which word in paragraph 1 means "ordinary"?
   A modern
   B different
   C bulging
   D average

3. Which paragraph tells how Neanderthals are related to modern humans?
   A 1
   B 2
   C 3
   D 4

4. You can conclude from the article that Neanderthals were more advanced than animals because they _____.
   A buried their dead
   B survived a harsh environment
   C lifted more weight than the average human
   D lived at the same time as Cro-Magnon people

5. *Harsh* can have the following meanings. Mark the meaning used in paragraph 2.
   A lacking in appeal
   B unpleasant to the ear
   C having a rough surface
   D physically discomforting

6. As you can tell from the article, scientists don't really know what happened to the Neanderthals. There are many ideas, but none have been proven. What's your idea? How could a strong and intelligent people like the Neanderthals just disappear?

Why doesn't the sun burn up?

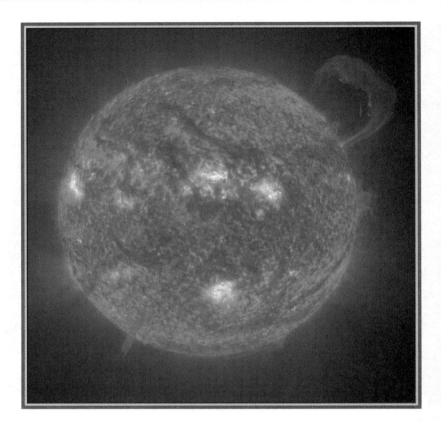

1. Scientists know that the sun is a star burning with fiery gases. They have watched hot currents of gas rise like fountains from inside the sun. These gas jets shoot out into space and then fall back. Scientists also know that the sun mostly burns hydrogen gas. Will the sun ever use up its fuel? Will it ever go out?

2. The center of the sun is tightly packed with gas particles, or atoms. It is also unbelievably hot. There the temperature is about 27 million degrees Fahrenheit, or 15 million degrees Celsius. Together, the pressure and the heat create nuclear reactions. The gas atoms split and join together into new atoms. As they do this, the atoms give off a great amount of heat and light. The sun is like a hydrogen bomb that keeps on exploding.

3. Even a tiny amount of nuclear fuel creates a lot of energy. The sun is so big that it could hold over a million Earths. Its atomic fuel has kept it burning for more than five billion years. It will also keep the sun burning for billions of years to come. Yet it is true that sometime in the far distant future the sun could use up all its gases. It could burn itself out.

4. The end of the sun would mean the end of life on Earth. But the sun isn't the only blazing star in the sky. Maybe by the time Earth's sun grows cold, people will have settled on another planet near a still brightly burning sun.

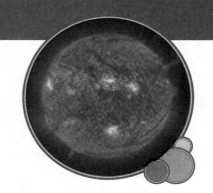

Circle the correct answer for questions 1–5.
Write your answer to question 6 on a separate piece of paper.

1. The article does *not* tell about the _____ of the sun.
    A   nuclear reactions
    B   incredible heat
    C   burning gases
    D   dark spots

2. Which word in paragraph 2 means "break apart"?
    A   create
    B   split
    C   join
    D   give

3. Which paragraph compares the size of the sun to Earth?
    A   1
    B   2
    C   3
    D   4

4. The sun will continue to burn for billions of years mainly because of its _____.
    A   fiery gases
    B   atomic fuel
    C   high temperature
    D   position in the solar system

5. You can conclude from the article that _____.
    A   nuclear fuel cannot create energy
    B   the sun is the largest star in the sky
    C   the sun won't burn up during our lives
    D   no other stars shine as brightly as the sun

6. Write a short story about what Earth will be like when the sun finally begins to burn out. How will people live? What animals will be affected first?

Did Atlantis really exist?

1   In the 300s B.C., a Greek philosopher named Plato wrote about an advanced civilization on an island continent. He called it Atlantis. Its people lived in peace. They were traders, sailors, and artists. Young people took part in a game with bulls. They wrestled with and jumped over the strong animals. Sadly, Plato wrote, the people grew overly proud about themselves. The gods decided to punish them. Suddenly, a great flood sank their island. In one day and one night, their civilization vanished.

2   Plato based his story on an earlier Egyptian legend. But could Atlantis have been more than just a story about a remarkable civilization? Could it have been a real place?

3   The island of Santorini lies in the Mediterranean Sea about 70 miles north of the island of Crete. It is now a collapsed volcano. But once it was Thera, part of the brilliant Minoan civilization centered on Crete. In 1470 B.C., the volcano exploded, setting off earthquakes and tidal waves. The terrible eruption hurled seven cubic miles of dust, rock, and deadly gases into the air above the Earth.

4   Temperatures dropped throughout the Northern Hemisphere. Food grew scarce. People left their homes in search of better ones. Experts don't know the exact year of the Thera eruption, although scientific detective work can help. Tree-ring dating in Ireland and California shows unusually cold years after 1470 B.C. And ice layers in Greenland have volcanic ash from about the same time.

5   King Minos's palace at Knossos on Crete also provides clues. When parts were dug up, wonderful wall paintings showed the bullfighting game that Plato wrote about. Also, no tools or pictures of war were found. People may never have all the answers, but Atlantis could have been real—really Crete and Thera.

Circle the correct answer for questions 1–5.
Write your answer to question 6 on a separate piece of paper.

1. The island of Thera is known today as _____.
   A Crete
   B Ireland
   C Santorini
   D Greenland

2. Which word in paragraph 3 means "caved in"?
   A tidal
   B centered
   C collapsed
   D exploded

3. Which paragraph tells about the effects of Thera's eruption?
   A 1
   B 2
   C 3
   D 4

4. What did *not* happen after Thera erupted?
   A war
   B tidal waves
   C earthquakes
   D dropping temperatures

5. You can conclude from the article that the eruption of Thera _____.
   A is only a legend
   B was written about at the time
   C left evidence around the world
   D was shown in paintings at Minos's palace

6. You have been asked to give a speech to the local historical society. Your job is to convince them that Atlantis really existed on the islands of Crete and Thera. Write your speech. Use facts from the article to support your case.

Can ants live in trees?

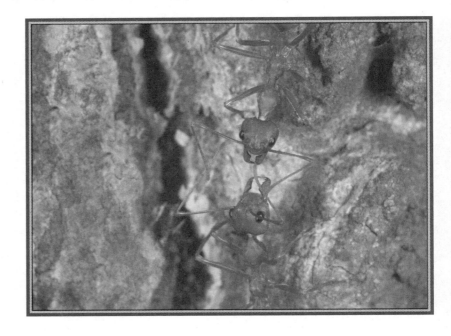

1   The open plains of Africa are home to a tree called the whistling thorn acacia. The name comes from the tree's long thorns and the sound the wind makes as it blows through the branches. The whistling thorn acacia looks unusual because its bark swells, forming knobs that are hollow inside.

2   An African ant, called the acacia ant, makes its home in these knobs. An acacia tree may have as many as 20,000 ants living in it. In exchange for room and board, the ants protect the tree from animals. Any animal that tries to eat acacia leaves soon finds its face covered with hundreds of biting, stinging ants.

3   Giraffes are the only animals that will approach a whistling thorn acacia. They have long tongues that can loop around the leaves. They pull leaves into their mouths without getting their faces near the tree. The giraffes don't seem to mind that their food is covered with thorns and ants. But even giraffes will only eat a few leaves from each tree.

4   Besides giving them a home, the acacia also feeds its ants. The leaves make a sugar solution that is like the nectar of flowers. The solution drips out at the base of the leaves where the ants gather to eat. As the Africans say, "God is good to the ants for giving them such a safe home. God is good to the tree for giving it such a fearsome army."

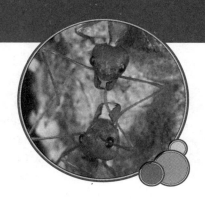

Circle the correct answer for questions 1–5.
Write your answer to question 6 on a separate piece of paper.

1. _____ are the only animals that eat acacia leaves.
   A Ants
   B Giraffes
   C Leopards
   D Elephants

2. Which word in paragraph 4 means "a sweet liquid produced by a plant"?
   A solution
   B nectar
   C acacia
   D base

3. Which paragraph tells how the whistling thorn acacia tree got its name?
   A 1
   B 2
   C 3
   D 4

4. The home of the acacia ant is created by _____.
   A long thorns
   B swollen bark
   C dripping leaves
   D hungry giraffes

5. You can conclude from the article that giraffes aren't affected by the acacia ant mostly because of their _____.
   A long neck
   B long tongue
   C pointed head
   D strong mouth

6. How is the relationship between acacia ants and the whistling thorn acacia similar to the relationship between bees and flowers? How is it different?

How can the San people live in the desert?

1. Africa's Kalahari (kah•lah•HAR•ee) Desert is a dry wilderness. The land provides little water, food, or shelter. Many people would not be able to survive there. Yet for hundreds of years, this desert has been home to a group of people called the San.

2. The San need special skills to survive in the Kalahari. They shield their skin from the sun by rubbing themselves with oil. Dust sticks to the oil and blocks out the sun's rays. These desert people also have unusual ways to get and store water. After carefully choosing a likely spot, they thrust a long, hollow reed into the ground. Then they suck on the reed, slowly drawing up water from under the ground. The San store extra water in shells from ostrich eggs. They bury this emergency water supply to keep the sun from drying it out.

3. Hunting and gathering food are also difficult in the Kalahari Desert. But with their skills, the San can hunt and collect a day's food in about two hours. The women find wild potatoes, roots, and fruits. For meat, the San will eat small desert creatures, like lizards and insects. But if a large animal is near, the men hunt it. Covered in leaves and feathers, they creep close to their game. Then they kill it with poison-tipped arrows. No part of the animal is wasted. The meat is eaten and the skin used for clothing. The stomach is made into a water bag.

4. Today, modern life has caught up with the San. Other people have taken some of their lands. Many San have gone to live in more settled areas. But there are still a few who follow their traditional way of life.

Circle the correct answer for questions 1–5.
Write your answer to question 6 on a separate piece of paper.

1. The article does *not* tell about the _____ of the San.

   A food

   B homes

   C water supply

   D poison arrows

2. Which word in paragraph 2 means "having to do with an unexpected event that calls for quick action"?

   A emergency   C hollow

   B unusual   D extra

3. Which paragraph tells where the Kalahari Desert is?

   A 1   C 3

   B 2   D 4

4. You can infer from the article that the San people _____.

   A use modern hunting methods

   B have no way to leave the area

   C spend all day searching for food

   D have the skills to survive in other climates

5. *Game* can have the following meanings. Mark the meaning used in paragraph 3.

   A a sports contest

   B ready for anything

   C a plan for reaching a goal

   D wild animals being hunted

6. There are classic tales of people learning to survive with nothing but their wits to help them. *Robinson Crusoe* and *The Swiss Family Robinson* are two such stories. Imagine that you are stranded in an environment completely different from what you're used to. Write a short story in which you describe your new environment and your experiences learning to survive in it.

Are birds really descended from dinosaurs?

1   During the 1980s, science came up with many new theories about dinosaurs. There were new ideas about how they moved and how they became extinct. Some scientists suggested that dinosaurs were not even reptiles. They might have been warm-blooded animals rather than cold-blooded.

2   One new theory is that today's birds are descended from dinosaurs. Not all scientists, however, are convinced that this is true. Some small meat-eating dinosaurs did have birdlike skeletons. They laid eggs in nests and took care of their young. But these facts do not *prove* a connection between dinosaurs and birds.

3   Then in 1996, scientists working in China dug up a bird skeleton. At least, that's what they thought at first. Looking closer, they decided it was a feathered dinosaur. They called it Sinosauropteryx (seye•no•sor•OP•tuh•riks) —"Chinese feathered lizard." The skeleton was about 130 million years old. True birds already existed on Earth at that time. But Sinosauropteryx and modern birds may have had a common ancestor.

4   A year later, another birdlike dinosaur was found in Argentina. This one was a seven-foot-long meat-eater. It had a birdlike hip structure and limbs that could flap like wings. The creature was about 90 million years old. It too may have shared a common ancestor with birds.

5   Of course, that's what the scientists who discovered it believe. Other scientists are not so certain. They aren't sure about Sinosauropteryx, either. Science may yet find a dinosaur that is undoubtedly a bird ancestor. Until that happens, it can't be definitely proven that the dinosaur–bird idea is true. That's the way science works.

Circle the correct answer for questions 1–5.
Write your answer to question 6 on a separate piece of paper.

1. Sinosauropteryx was discovered in _____.
   A Chile
   B China
   C Australia
   D Argentina

2. Which word in paragraph 2 means "sure beyond a doubt"?
   A connection
   B descended
   C convinced
   D prove

3. Which paragraph tells about the discovery in Argentina?
   A 1
   B 2
   C 3
   D 4

4. You can conclude from the article that scientists _____.
   A cannot agree that today's birds are descended from dinosaurs
   B cannot find a resemblance between birds and dinosaurs
   C agree that a feathered dinosaur must be a bird
   D agree that all dinosaurs were reptiles

5. *Common* can have the following meanings. Mark the meaning used in paragraph 3.
   A coarse
   B ordinary
   C happening often
   D shared by two things

6. Take a position that dinosaurs and birds either are or are not related and write a short paper to persuade scientists to support your belief.

What is the legend of the phoenix?

1   People in ancient times saw things die in the fall and come alive again in the spring. They watched the sun die in its own flames each night only to rise anew in the morning. All this made them think about the mystery of life and death. Storytellers tried to explain these thoughts in the legend of the phoenix (FEE•niks).

2   The phoenix was a beautiful red and gold bird with a sweet voice. According to most stories, only one phoenix lived on Earth at a time. It was always a male bird. The fabulous creature lived for 500 years. Then it built a nest of twigs from spice trees. Setting the nest on fire, the phoenix let the flames burn up its body. From the ashes rose a fully grown phoenix, just as beautiful as the last. The new phoenix gathered up the ashes of the old. Then it flew to the City of the Sun to lay them on the altar of the sun god. After living out its 500 years, the new phoenix repeated the cycle.

3   The ancient Greeks and Egyptians often told this story about the never-ending gift of life. The phoenix became a symbol of rebirth. It also stands for a promise. No matter how final something may seem, it could be the beginning of something else as beautiful as what has gone before.

Circle the correct answer for questions 1–5.
Write your answer to question 6 on a separate piece of paper.

1. The most important fact about the phoenix was that it _____.
   A was a male bird
   B had a sweet voice
   C had red and gold feathers
   D rose from the ashes of a dead phoenix

2. Which word in paragraph 2 means "did over again in the same way"?
   A rose
   B lived
   C gathered
   D repeated

3. What happened first in the life of the phoenix?
   A It gathered up ashes.
   B It built a nest of twigs.
   C It let flames burn its body.
   D It flew to the City of the Sun.

4. What did *not* make ancient people think about life and death?
   A plants blossoming in the spring and dying in the fall
   B clouds moving through the sky
   C the sun rising and setting
   D the legend of the phoenix

5. You can infer from the article that the phoenix probably _____.
   A was connected with sun worship
   B ate fruit in order to live so long
   C was fascinated by fires
   D did not sing often

6. Think of something that could be a symbol of rebirth and write your own tale about it.

What is the Mariana Trench?

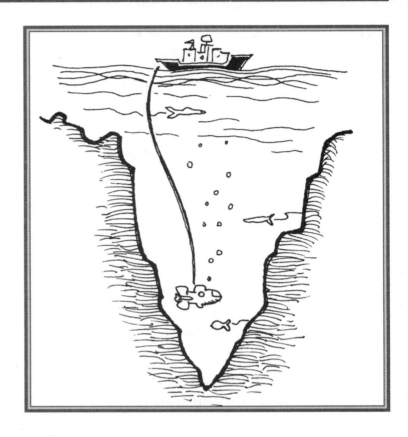

1   In 1951, a research ship was charting the ocean floor near the Mariana Islands in the Pacific Ocean. The scientists on board were using echo sounders. These instruments bounce signals off the ocean floor. They were showing water depths of between two and three miles. Suddenly, they showed a depth of almost seven miles. The scientists were astounded. Even the Grand Canyon is only one mile deep. They named the watery canyon the Mariana Trench.

2   The Mariana Trench is the deepest ever measured. It is one of a long chain of trenches in the middle of the Pacific Ocean. All the trenches are very narrow, deep, and dark. The water is very cold there and has a pressure of more than eight tons per square inch. Can anything live at such depths and under such pressure?

3   In 1960, two men found the answer to this question. They went down into the Mariana Trench in a special underwater vessel. It had been designed to endure the great pressures of those depths. The men went down seven miles to the trench floor. Turning on a searchlight, they looked through a porthole. A fish swam peacefully in front of them. Their trip took nine hours. But it proved that life does exist in the incredible depths of the Mariana Trench.

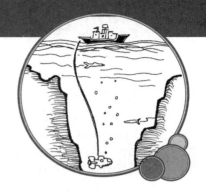

Circle the correct answer for questions 1–5.
Write your answer to question 6 on a separate piece of paper.

1. The trenches in the Pacific Ocean are *not* _____.
   A shallow
   B narrow
   C cold
   D dark

2. Which word in paragraph 3 means "to survive or put up with great hardship"?
   A exist
   B endure
   C proved
   D designed

3. What event happened last in the article?
   A Life was seen on the trench floor.
   B The Mariana Trench was named.
   C Men explored the area in an underwater vessel.
   D A research ship charted the floor of the Pacific Ocean.

4. You can infer from the article that _____.
   A there are no trenches in the Atlantic Ocean
   B a deeper trench will never be found
   C fish can survive high water pressure
   D echo sounders are always reliable

5. *Chain* can have the following meanings. Mark the meaning used in paragraph 2.
   A a series of connected things
   B a rope of metal links or rings
   C a unit of length equal to 66 feet
   D stores under the same ownership

6. Would you like to explore the ocean floor? Why or why not? What would you want to learn about it?

What is the Iditarod?

1 Alaskans call the Iditarod "the last great race." It's a sled dog race that follows the Iditarod Trail, an old mail and shipping route in Alaska. Every year, dozens of brave men and women and their dog teams compete in this grueling race. Not everyone manages to finish.

2 The race begins on the first Saturday in March. Every two minutes, a dog team and its driver speed away from Anchorage. Their goal is Nome, a town more than 1,000 miles away. To get there, the teams must cross two mountain ranges and the frozen Yukon River. They race over long stretches of empty wilderness. Along the way, the teams face plenty of danger. Angry moose may attack the dogs. Fierce blizzards can hit suddenly. Temperatures as low as 40° below zero exhaust dogs and drivers alike.

3 Like athletes, the best teams practice for the race all year. Drivers work to build up their animals' speed and strength. The dogs must have the endurance for a race that can last ten or more days.

4 The teams don't cover the whole distance without stopping. They must sign in at 27 checkpoints along the route. There they eat and rest. Drivers also check their dogs then to be sure they are still healthy. A hurt or sick dog may not continue. At the stops, each team's time is recorded. And the team with the best time wins.

Circle the correct answer for questions 1–5.
Write your answer to question 6 on a separate piece of paper.

1. The Iditarod takes place in _____.

   A Russia

   B Alaska

   C Canada

   D Minnesota

2. Which word in paragraph 1 means "exhausting or punishing"?

   A great

   B brave

   C grueling

   D shipping

3. Which paragraph tells about the course of the race?

   A 1

   B 2

   C 3

   D 4

4. Which of these would *not* cause a problem for teams in the Iditarod?

   A frigid temperatures

   B fierce blizzards

   C angry wildlife

   D lack of food

5. *Check* can have the following meanings. Mark the meaning used in paragraph 4.

   A to bring to a stop

   B to look over carefully

   C a written draft on a bank

   D a mark to show that something is correct

6. Imagine you are working at one of the checkpoints on the Iditarod route. Write about what you would see and do over the course of a day. Use information from the article to describe the conditions of the drivers and their teams.

What causes avalanches?

1.   An avalanche is a mass of snow or ice that slides rapidly down a steep slope. Long ago, people thought that avalanches were caused by an angry god or by a dragon lashing its tail under the Earth. Today scientists tell us that snow can break loose for many reasons.

2.   A strong winter wind can cause an avalanche, blowing down huge quantities of fine, dry snow. More often, though, the weight of the snow itself is the cause. A mass of snow on a mountain ledge grows larger and larger as winter snows pile up. Then warmer weather comes. The snow melts and freezes over and over again. This makes the rock ledge weak or the snow loose. In either case, the weight of the snow becomes too much for the base. The whole mass thunders down the mountain.

3.   Sound can also cause an avalanche. Sound waves from a voice or another noise set up vibrations. These vibrations can cause the snow particles in loosely packed snow to vibrate, too. The snow shakes itself loose, and tons of it plunge down the slope. Sometimes gunfire or explosives are used deliberately to start small avalanches before the snow drifts get dangerously big.

4.   An avalanche travels at the speed of an express train, swallowing everything in its path. At last it comes to rest, a frightening mass of snow, trees, houses, and sometimes people. No wonder the Swiss call an avalanche the "white killer."

Circle the correct answer for questions 1–5.
Write your answer to question 6 on a separate piece of paper.

1. The article does *not* tell about _____ an avalanche.
   A the causes of
   B what to do in
   C the Swiss name for
   D the weight of snow in

2. Which word in paragraph 3 means "on purpose"?
   A dangerously
   B deliberately
   C vibrations
   D loosely

3. Which paragraph tells how sound starts avalanches?
   A 1
   B 2
   C 3
   D 4

4. Which of the following is *not* a common cause of an avalanche?
   A sound
   B hail storms
   C strong wind
   D weight of the snow

5. You can conclude from the article that avalanches _____.
   A contain only wet snow
   B began to happen in recent years
   C don't happen in warmer weather
   D have caused problems in Switzerland

6. Several years ago, avalanches struck mountain villages in France and Austria. Parts of towns were destroyed, and more than 50 people lost their lives. If you lived in one of these towns, would you want to rebuild your home? Explain why or why not.

What are kachinas?

1   To the Hopi people, *kachinas* are spirits. Kachinas play an important part in the culture of these Native Americans. The Hopi believe the spirits are connected to the seasons of the year. During the cold months, the kachinas live under the ground in mountains far away. Then, as the earth warms and plants begin to grow again, the spirits return. The kachinas live among the Hopi in the growing season.

2   During this time of the year, the Hopi people celebrate with many festivals. To recognize the kachinas' importance, they portray the spirits in their ceremonies. Adult men put on masks and costumes to act as kachinas. There are about 250 different kachinas. They take the shapes of animals, evil demons, and clowns. Each kachina has a special personality and role.

3   The year begins in February with Powamu, a planting ceremony. The Crow Mother kachina brings gifts and sprouting beans to her people. In July, there is Niman, the Home Dance. This is the last ceremony of the year. In it, the kachinas get ready to return to their mountain homes.

4   Hopi children are expected to learn the roles the kachinas play. To help them, adults carve kachina dolls. Each one is decorated as a particular spirit. Then they are hung on the walls of homes. In this way, kachina dolls remind the children of their culture.

Circle the correct answer for questions 1–5.
Write your answer to question 6 on a separate piece of paper.

1. In festivals, the parts of kachinas are acted by _____.
   A adult women
   B adult men
   C children
   D spirits

2. Which word in paragraph 2 means "to play the role of"?
   A celebrate
   B recognize
   C portray
   D masks

3. Which paragraph tells how Hopi children learn about kachinas?
   A 1
   B 2
   C 3
   D 4

4. What is the main idea of the article?
   A Kachinas are spirits that play an important role in the Hopi culture.
   B The Hopi people recognize the kachinas' importance in ceremonies.
   C Kachinas return in the spring and live among the Hopi.
   D Kachina dolls teach Hopi children about their culture.

5. *Seasons* can have the following meanings. Mark the meaning used in paragraph 1.
   A flavors
   B times of the year
   C in sports, periods of playing games
   D treats to make ready for use, as wood

6. Why do you think so many cultures around the world have ceremonies that center around the planting and harvesting of crops?

What is amber?

1   Millions of years ago, there were great forests of pine trees. Just as they do today, the trees oozed a sticky substance called resin. This material was a tree's way of fighting insects. Bugs crawling on the bark were trapped in the resin and died. With the insects inside, the yellow drops grew hard.

2   In time, the trees died and rotted away. But the resin did not decay. Buried in the soil, it grew harder until it looked like a stone. Over millions of years, it became a fossil that is called amber.

3   For thousands of years, amber has been prized as a gem. It may be clear or cloudy, and its color may be yellow, orange, brown, red, white, blue, green, or even black. Amber is not like diamonds or other mineral gems. It is very light and warm to the touch. It can also pick up an electrical charge. Because of that, people long ago thought amber held magic. They believed that the beautiful golden drops came from the sun.

4   Amber is still popular for jewelry today. But its greatest value is to scientists. Pieces of amber containing animal or plant matter are time capsules. In them, scientists have examined ants, spiders, leaves, and feathers. All of these things are millions of years old. In most fossils, the living matter has turned to stone. But in amber, scientists can look at the original cells.

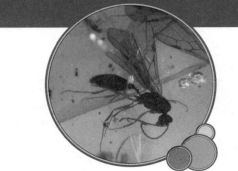

Circle the correct answer for questions 1–5.
Write your answer to question 6 on a separate piece of paper.

1. Amber is a product of _____.
   A insects
   B sunlight
   C scientists
   D pine trees

2. Which word in paragraph 4 means "the smallest parts that make up living plants and animals"?
   A cells
   B fossils
   C pieces
   D capsules

3. Which paragraph tells why people long ago thought amber held magic?
   A 1
   B 2
   C 3
   D 4

4. What happens last when amber is formed?
   A Resin becomes a fossil.
   B Resin becomes hard.
   C A tree oozes resin.
   D Bugs die in resin.

5. You can conclude from the article that amber _____.
   A is still being made today
   B will never be made again
   C doesn't take long to get hard
   D is made by trees other than pines

6. Write a one- or two-paragraph summary of the article you just read.

What was Lake Missoula?

1   Missoula, Montana, lies near the Rocky Mountains. Above the city, the bare rock on the mountains is lined with curious horizontal stripes. There are dozens of them.

2   Hundreds of miles west, near Spokane, Washington, lie the Channeled Scablands. This is a region of deep, dry canyons, pools, and huge waterfalls without water. There are heaps of soil and gravel, called moraines, that are hundreds of feet high. On the canyon walls are stripes like those above Missoula.

3   From an airplane, this land looks like it was formed by water erosion. But the river that formed it would have had to be 1,500 feet deep and hundreds of miles wide. It would have carried ten times the water of all the rivers in the world together.

4   In fact, this is exactly what happened—not once, but many times. About 15,000 years ago, during the last great ice age, a lake covered much of western Montana. Scientists call it Lake Missoula. It contained about as much water as Lakes Erie and Ontario combined. This estimate is based on the lake's shorelines—those stripes above Missoula today.

5   The lake was held back by a dam of ice in what is now Idaho. As the Earth grew warmer, the ice melted. Eventually, the dam broke, sending 500 cubic miles of water rushing downstream. It ground down everything in its path. It carved out valleys, jumped mountains, and dumped enormous boulders hundreds of miles away. It flooded the site of Portland, Oregon, and finally burst into the sea. After a few days, the flood was over. Meanwhile, back at Lake Missoula, a new ice dam was forming.

Circle the correct answer for questions 1–5.
Write your answer to question 6 on a separate piece of paper.

1. The ice dam that formed Lake Missoula was in today's state of _____.

   A Washington

   B Montana

   C Oregon

   D Idaho

2. Which word in paragraph 2 means "deep, narrow valleys with steep sides"?

   A heaps

   B canyons

   C moraines

   D waterfalls

3. Which paragraph tells about the size of Lake Missoula?

   A 1

   B 2

   C 3

   D 4

4. The Lake Missoula flood was caused by _____.

   A an ice age

   B a broken dam

   C huge waterfalls

   D enormous boulders

5. You can conclude from the article that scientists can tell how many Lake Missoula floods there were from _____.

   A fossils found nearby

   B the volume of water

   C the stripes in the canyon

   D rocks dumped downstream

6. Suppose people had been around to witness a Lake Missoula flood. Write a myth that they might have passed down to explain the flood.

Do llamas live only in South America?

1   You are hiking in the mountains of California. In the distance, a group of people leading pack horses is coming toward you. But what strange-looking horses they are! They have long necks. Their coats are shaggy. As they come closer, you stare in surprise. The horses are *llamas!*

2   Llamas are native to South America, but North American ranchers have been keeping them for about 100 years. Today there are more than 50,000 llamas in the United States. Some people keep them as pets. Others use them as pack animals. They are bred for mountain travel, and they can carry up to 200 pounds. A few ranchers raise llamas for their wool or for their meat, just as South Americans have for thousands of years.

3   Ranchers are increasingly breeding llamas as guard animals. This is because of another animal that has spread across the United States—the coyote. This wild creature once was common only in the West. Recently, its numbers have grown throughout the eastern states, too. Coyotes often raid farms and towns to eat. They kill pets and livestock.

4   Sheep ranchers in particular have problems with coyotes. Their favorite food is lamb. But when llamas guard the flock, few lambs are lost. When a coyote appears, llamas give a warning cry. Then they chase the coyote away or kick it with their sharp hooves.

5   Llamas are more effective guard animals than dogs. They can be trained more quickly. They live longer. And they don't have to be fed every day. They graze in the pasture along with the sheep.

Circle the correct answer for questions 1–5.
Write your answer to question 6 on a separate piece of paper.

1. About how much weight can a llama carry?
   A 100 pounds
   B 150 pounds
   C 200 pounds
   D 250 pounds

2. Which word in paragraph 3 means "more and more"?
   A only
   B recently
   C throughout
   D increasingly

3. Which paragraph tells why llamas are better than dogs for guarding sheep?
   A 1
   B 2
   C 3
   D 5

4. What is *not* a reason why ranchers are breeding llamas as guard animals?
   A Llamas scare away coyotes.
   B Llamas can be trained quickly.
   C Llamas take up less space than dogs.
   D Llamas don't have to be fed every day.

5. You can conclude from the article that llamas _____.
   A chase away sheep
   B have many worthwhile uses
   C are raised mainly for their meat
   D are a popular pet in the United States

6. Write an advertisement to promote the llama as a great family pet. Be sure to highlight all the positive uses that people would find appealing.

What was Manzanar?

1   On the morning of December 7, 1941, Jeanne Wakatsuki and her sisters stood near the coast at Long Beach, California. The young children were watching their father's fishing boat move out to sea. Suddenly, the boat turned back. The girls waited anxiously to find out why. Just then, a man running along the dock yelled, "The Japanese have bombed Pearl Harbor!" The surprise bombing of the navy base in Hawaii meant that the United States and Japan were now at war.

2   Mr. Wakatsuki was a native of Japan. His children, though, had been born in the United States. They all thought of themselves as Americans. But with a war on, people began to distrust Japanese Americans. The U.S. government acted quickly. It took away the homes and businesses of the Wakatsuki family and thousands of other Japanese Americans. Then it sent them to an internment camp called Manzanar in the high, chilly Sierra Nevada mountains.

3   At first, Manzanar was a crude and poorly equipped place. Gradually, the Japanese Americans built schools and beautiful rock gardens. Jeanne Wakatsuki and the other children studied and hiked in the mountains. Yet, like all the residents of Manzanar, they had no freedom. For three years, they were not allowed to leave camp.

4   Much later Jeanne Wakatsuki wrote a book about Manzanar. By then, the U.S. government realized its mistake. The government finally agreed to pay the Japanese Americans for the damage done. But there was really no way to make up for the years that Manzanar stole from loyal U.S. citizens like the Wakatsukis.

Circle the correct answer for questions 1–5.
Write your answer to question 6 on a separate piece of paper.

1. The Wakatsukis lived in _____.
   A Japan
   B Hawaii
   C New York
   D California

2. Which word in paragraph 2 means "state of being held against one's will"?
   A war
   B camp
   C native
   D internment

3. Which paragraph tells how Jeanne found out a war had started?
   A 1
   B 2
   C 3
   D 4

4. You can conclude from the article that the U.S. government _____.
   A took responsibility for maintaining internment camps
   B paid Japanese Americans generous amounts of money
   C recognized later that it treated Japanese Americans unfairly
   D allowed Japanese Americans freedom to leave internment camps

5. *Coast* can have the following meanings. Mark the meaning used in paragraph 1.
   A land near a shore
   B get by with no effort
   C immediate area of view
   D move easily without power

6. What is an internment camp? Write one or two paragraphs to answer this question. Use information from the article in your answer.

What is the truth about piranhas?

1   About 20 kinds of fish called piranhas live in the streams of South America. Their sides are silvery and their bellies are yellow or red. Their backs may be green, blue, or black. The smallest ones are fully grown at 4 inches. Larger ones may grow up to 18 inches long.

2   The bigger piranhas have a very bad reputation. But they seem to deserve it. Even though piranhas will eat bread and fruit used as bait, they mostly dine on other fish. Sometimes they even eat each other. That's why they are also known as cannibal fish.

3   Triangle-shaped teeth line the strong jaws of the piranha. These teeth are sharp and can slash off pieces of flesh with lightning speed. Piranhas devour their food in no time at all. They usually choose an animal that is hurt or weak. When the fish attack, the water around them foams and churns. Then in just a few minutes, the water grows still again. Little is left of the victim. The flesh has been stripped from the bones.

4   Yet piranhas don't always act this way. Sometimes they ignore people and animals in the water around them. No one is certain why they attack at one time and not at another. The water level and temperature, the time of year, or the food supply might make the difference. The truth about the piranha seems to be that it is as changeable as it is dangerous.

Circle the correct answer for questions 1–5.
Write your answer to question 6 on a separate piece of paper.

1. Piranhas _____.
   A eat only people
   B never eat bread or fruit
   C sometimes eat each other
   D will always attack an animal

2. Which word in paragraph 3 means "eat greedily"?
   A slash
   B devour
   C choose
   D attack

3. Which paragraph tells what piranhas look like?
   A 1
   B 2
   C 3
   D 4

4. If an animal is eaten by a piranha, it is likely that it was _____.
   A injured
   B floating
   C paddling
   D very small

5. You can conclude from the article that a piranha _____.
   A is predictable about what it attacks
   B is particular about what it eats
   C could survive in the ocean
   D cannot be trusted

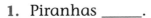

6. In a food chain, energy and nutrients are passed from one organism to another. Explain the piranha's role in the food chain and explain why this fish is important in this process.

What was mysterious about the Roanoke Island colony?

1. One of America's first colonies disappeared mysteriously—not just once, but twice. The English landed on Roanoke Island off the coast of North Carolina in the late 1500s. This first group just explored the island. They drew maps and wrote descriptions. But because food was scarce, they soon sailed back to England. Shortly afterward, the supply ship they had been waiting for reached Roanoke. Fifteen men from that ship decided to settle there.

2. A year later, another ship carrying settlers stopped at Roanoke. These people found the settlement deserted and overgrown with plants. One man's skeleton was discovered, but there was no trace of the others. Even so, the new settlers decided to rebuild the colony. They had some happy times. They celebrated the birth of Virginia Dare, the first English child born in America. But they also had bad times. There was not enough food. Unfriendly natives were a danger. Diseases killed many people. Finally, one of the leaders went back to England for help.

3. Years passed before the leader could return to Roanoke. As his ship reached the island, people on board shouted and played music. There was no reply. A landing party found some rusted armor and damaged papers, but no settlers. The only clue was the word *Croatoan* carved in a tree. Perhaps the settlers had moved to Croatoan Island. Yet no sign of them was ever found there or anywhere else. To this day, the fate of the Roanoke settlers remains a mystery.

Circle the correct answer for questions 1–5.
Write your answer to question 6 on a separate piece of paper.

1. The first English group sailed back to England because they were _____.
   A frightened by the natives
   B tired of exploring
   C in need of food
   D lonely

2. Which word in paragraph 2 means "left empty"?
   A stopped
   B deserted
   C discovered
   D celebrated

3. What event happened last in the history of the Roanoke Island colony?
   A The word *Croatoan* was found carved on a tree.
   B The first supply ship reached Roanoke Island.
   C Settlers celebrated the birth of Virginia Dare.
   D Settlers explored the island and drew maps.

4. You can infer from the article that _____.
   A new settlers had mostly happy times
   B Croatoan Island became a popular colonial settlement
   C colonial settlements were not recognized by England
   D other colonial settlements disappeared because of harsh conditions

5. *Trace* can have the following meanings. Mark the meaning used in paragraph 2.
   A a track or sign left behind
   B to follow step by step
   C to make one's way
   D to copy carefully

6. Imagine that you are the last survivor on Roanoke Island. You want to let people in England know what happened to your group. Write a letter about your experiences and tell what you're going to do now.

What is a coelacanth?

1   The coelacanth (SEE•luh•kanth) is a prehistoric ancestor of today's bony fish. Scientists had studied fossils of this strange fish but never dreamed of seeing a live one. They thought the coelacanth died out 65 million years ago.

2   Then in 1938, a large, oily fish was caught in a net off the coast of East Africa. About five feet long and 150 pounds, its body was covered with round, blue scales flecked with white. Its large tail had a small fin on it. But strangest of all were its four other strong fins. They could rotate and looked more like flippers or legs than fins.

3   In port, the head of a nearby museum heard about the unusual catch. She quickly called in an expert to identify the dead, smelly fish. "This is a coelacanth," the excited scientist said. "It's a living fossil!"

4   News of the strange find flashed around the world. A reward was offered for catching another coelacanth. In 1952, a second fish was finally caught near the Comoro Islands of Africa. Since then, scientists have studied the coelacanth in deep ocean caves where their coloring acts as a camouflage. The fish appear to leave the caves at the same time every afternoon to find food. One puzzle that scientists haven't been able to solve, though, is where the young coelacanths are.

5   In 1998, coelacanths were found off the coast of Indonesia, more than 6,000 miles from the Comoro Islands. These fish are brown with gold flecks, but that seems to be the only difference between them and their African "cousins." Further study of "Old Fourlegs" may help scientists find out how these fish survived for millions of years without changing.

Circle the correct answer for questions 1–5.
Write your answer to question 6 on a separate piece of paper.

1. The coelacanth _____.
   A is a small fish
   B is very common
   C lives in shallow waters
   D has existed for millions of years

2. Which word in paragraph 4 means "a disguise to help in hiding"?
   A puzzle
   B reward
   C coloring
   D camouflage

3. Which paragraph tells where the first living coelacanth was found?
   A 1
   B 2
   C 3
   D 4

4. What did *not* happen after the coelacanth was caught in 1938?
   A It was identified by an expert.
   B More were found off the coast of India.
   C Scientists studied the fish in deep ocean caves.
   D A reward was offered for catching another one.

5. You can probably infer that the coelacanth is called "Old Fourlegs" because _____.
   A it walked on land 65 million years ago
   B it walks along the ocean bottom
   C its four fins look like legs
   D it's related to the sea lion

6. The coelacanth has been around for 410 million years. What is your theory about the survival of this fish? Give reasons for your ideas.

Do old songs hold secret codes?

1   "Swing low, sweet chariot, comin' for to carry me home...." Most people have heard this old song. It began as a slave spiritual, a hymn that African American slaves sang in the fields. Other slave spirituals that are still known today are "Follow the Drinking Gourd" and "Wade in the Water." What many people do not know is that these songs contained hidden codes. Slaves listening to them learned lessons that would help them escape to freedom.

2   To understand these codes, it helps to look closely at the words. Another word for "chariot" is "wagon." "The wagon" is one of many names that have been given to the constellation best known as the "Big Dipper." At the end of the Big Dipper's handle is the North Star. If slaves followed the North Star, it led them to the northern states, where they would be free. The "drinking gourd" also refers to the Big Dipper.

3   So, why does the song say "swing low"? Every 24 hours, the Big Dipper goes in a circle around the North Star. It is lowest in the sky at dusk. At that time, most slaves would be done with work for the day. No one would pay attention to where they were until morning. That meant that they would have all night to run before anyone started to chase them. Other songs gave more instructions. "Wade in the Water" told slaves to walk in streams. That way, dogs would lose their scent and not be able to follow them.

4   When slave owners heard slaves singing these songs in the fields, they did not worry. They thought that they were merely hymns. The slaves knew better and these songs became tools that carried them to freedom.

Circle the correct answer for questions 1–5.
Write your answer to question 6 on a separate piece of paper.

1. The chariot in the song is a symbol for _____.
   A a wagon slaves could hide in
   B the Big Dipper
   C a stream
   D a car

2. Which word in paragraph 1 means "religious song"?
   A hymn
   B gourd
   C lesson
   D code

3. Which paragraph tells why the slave owners did not tell the slaves to stop singing the songs?
   A 1
   B 2
   C 3
   D 4

4. You can infer from the article that _____.
   A escaping slavery was easy
   B slaves drank out of gourds
   C slave owners wanted slaves to escape
   D dogs were used to hunt escaped slaves

5. *Scent* can have the following meanings. Mark the meaning used in paragraph 3.
   A smell of a person
   B sense of smell
   C perfume
   D inkling

6. Imagine that you are an ex-slave who escaped. Write a journal entry describing how the words of the songs mentioned in the article helped you.

Can dogs smell cancer?

1   The power of a dog's nose is well known. For years, dogs have been employed to sniff out wild game, criminals, and illegal drugs. Now, doctors think they may have found yet another use for this keen sense of smell. Dogs may be able to smell cancer.

2   Cancer is one of the leading causes of death in the world. The disease can often be stopped if found early enough, but it can be hard to detect. While cancers are believed to have specific odors, the human nose is not nearly strong enough to smell them. This is where a dog might come in.

3   In the past, there have been many stories about dogs acting strangely around people who had cancer. In 1989, a woman said that her dog would not stop sniffing at a spot on her leg. Finally, she started to wonder if something was wrong and went to see a doctor. The spot turned out to be skin cancer.

4   More recently, doctors have done a number of studies. They think that dogs may be able to smell different forms of cancer on a person's breath. So far, the results have shown that the doctors may be right.

5   Many problems remain. A dog cannot tell a doctor what it is smelling. Also, dogs usually smell many things at once. It is hard to know if they are reacting to the cancer or to something else. Still, even if only a few lives are saved, dogs will have one more reason to be called man's best friend.

Circle the correct answer for questions 1–5.
Write your answer to question 6 on a separate piece of paper.

1. One problem with using dogs to detect cancer is that _____.
   A making dogs smell cancer is cruel
   B they cannot tell people what they smell
   C dogs cannot smell as well as people can
   D dogs behave strangely when they smell skin cancer

2. Which word in paragraph 1 means "used"?
   A employed
   B found
   C able
   D keen

3. Which paragraph tells about a specific case of a dog smelling cancer?
   A 1
   B 2
   C 3
   D 4

4. You can conclude from the article that _____.
   A doctors are still not sure that dogs can smell cancer
   B cats and other pets can probably smell cancer
   C doctors are very fond of dogs
   D skin cancer smells unpleasant

5. *Leading* can have the following meanings. Mark the meaning used in paragraph 2.
   A being the boss of
   B most common
   C influencing
   D best

6. What are some other things that dogs can do for people? Which do you think is most important?